Get Your Act Together

A 30-Day Accountability Journal

Get Your Act Together

A 30-Day Accountability Journal

JEFFREY T. TIERNEY

McGahan

Get Your Act Together & Accountability Journal

Copyright © 2021 by Jeffrey T. Tierney

MCGAHAN PUBLISHING HOUSE | LYNCHBURG, TN
www.mphbooks.com
Requests for information should be sent to:
info@mphbooks.com

_____

ISBN 978-1-951252-12-0

Contents

Acknowledgments

I would also like to thank Robyn Whaling for the inspiration to write this journal. She helped me get out of my comfort zone and helped me to believe in my ability that there might be a perspective that I could offer the world after some of the trials and tribulations that I had encountered in my life. I will be forever grateful to you for pushing me to do this journal. I hope it brings people closer to themselves, their loved ones, their spouses, and the Trinity.

I would like to thank Pastor George Garrett III for helping me sort through the Bible Verses to help make this journal a complete work. Without his guidance, I don't feel that this journal would have the effect needed to help take everyone into their hearts journey with the Holy Spirit for deep sanctification.

I would also like to thank my Pastor Andrew Burnett for his tireless work on refining my heart and letting Jesus bring me back from the dead. Your love and patience have meant everything to me on this journey.

Finally, I thank my good and dear friend Jennifer Lopez. You have taught me how important it is to speak with love and to still be direct at the same time. Because of your wisdom of this area, I have grown as man. Your advice has been valuable and will forever be appreciated more than you will ever know.

Finally, thank you to Brandon Ryan for guiding me to Caleb Poston for helping my dream come true.

"For our struggle is not against flesh and blood, but against the rulers, against the authorities, against the powers of this dark world and against the spiritual forces of evil in the heavenly realms."

Ephesians 6:12

For YC,

Thank you for teaching me how to be a man of excellence, of learning the skill of what true patience means, and what my identify in Christ in means. I will be forever grateful that we were in one another's lives and the lessons that I learned to become a man of love.

Finally, for the inspiration of getting me motivated to write this journal to help on their path to finding themselves through the Holy Spirit. I will be forever grateful.

Introduction

The intent of this journal is to help you in your daily walk toward being a Christ Centered individual, and to hear the Voice of the Holy Spirit. I had spent most of my young college life involved in parapsychology and transpersonal psychology and the better half of 20 years on the new age and eastern paths until I had a horrible experience during at a Shamanic Journeying conference that brought me back to Christ.

In my early college years, I understood how critical it was to take accountability for your wounded parts and the way that you interacted and treated others. However, during that time, I was not under the direction of Christ and the Holy Spirit. Don't get me wrong. I still loved Jesus, but I had been deceived into what the new age was teaching about Jesus. However, still I felt this burning desire regarding accountability must be an intrinsic or an innate idea that must come from within. It must be a consuming belief system that leads to work on yourself daily. To hold yourself accountable in your thoughts, words, and actions toward yourself and others.

Today, everyone wants a quick fix. I am guilty of this in my interactions toward others. I am a quick processor and I have always expected others to work on themselves and to be accountable to me like I am toward myself and them.

In my relationship with the woman who I loved deeply, was ready to purpose to and had gone through marriage class with, I was surprised how the lack of accountability could destroy something so good. The relationship ended because of fear, trauma, and misunderstanding. I was shown that people don't want to get their acts together for many reasons. The Spirit of Pride, fear, family systems, a past filled with extreme abuse of all forms: physical, mental, emotional, and sexual, generational curses, vows being made with the supernatural due to emotional hurts from previous partners, psychodynamic patterns of belief systems that are being played out in relationships, and spiritual warfare from Satan and the demonic. I am sure there are other reasons, but these are some of the main reasons that I have seen play out repeatedly in people's lives and that had played out in my relationship toward marriage, not to mention countless other relationships throughout the course of my life. This was truly a relationship that both of us were shown that God wanted to bless us with to serve each other and with some wonderful things for the rest of the world. Within an instant, due to all these things, it was destroyed. From this grief and pain, I wanted to help friends, lovers, spouses, families, business, and individuals improve themselves so the opportunity I had would never be wasted again.

We are living in a time where people in the church and on this planet are becoming less and less accountable. I see it every day in my job and the people I am surrounded with. I admit that I started to become bitter about this situation and I asked God about what I could do about it. He responded in a various number of ways. One, I had to continue to walk in my journey toward Christ and Him. I had to continue to be accountable for myself and my actions toward others, to live my man code so to speak. Secondly, I have been close to death through several health issues and I had to stop living from fear. Sometimes, in my relationships, I would see windows or visions of what people would need to do in their lives from the Holy Spirit to heal and I would get so excited that I would want to share. But sometimes, people aren't ready for these things. So I am having to learn when to share things and when not to share things. Thirdly, this isn't about perfection. God loves us unconditionally. God sees us perfectly. It isn't about telling someone how live their lives. This is hard lesson I have had to learn, especially with the woman I loved so deeply. However, in healthy relationships and a Christ centered relationship, both individuals can help one another become the best versions of themselves and with the help of the Holy Spirit, are able to grow closer to Christ and one another. I believe this is the reason why I am creating the Get Your Act Together and Accountability Journal.

We are living in a time where Satan is destroying relationships and marriages on this planet. We have become so immersed in technology that no one knows how to communicate heart to heart within anyone anymore. The divorce rate is at an all-time high of 61 percent and no one takes the covenant that they make with God or their marriage seriously anymore. The point of this journal is to start taking an inventory of yourself. Your thoughts, feelings, words, actions, and attitudes you have toward yourself and others. It is meant to take you toward Christ and others daily. It is meant to bring more love and joy into your life and to enhance more connection into your relationships and marriage. This isn't about beating yourself up or about striving for perfection. This about loving yourself and others more daily and listening to the Voice of the Holy Spirit to help yourself be gentle toward yourself more, and to have a servant's heart toward others. It is to help you face your deepest fears about yourself and to do the much needed emotional and soul wound work that you need to get yourself to let your Spirit lead the way.

Too many people are afraid to do the work on themselves and to let God heal them. This leaves the door open for Satan. We need to let the Holy Spirit heal our divided heart. We need more people in the body of Christ to have the courage to face themselves. Even if you don't believe in God or Christ, step up and start living accountable to yourself and the people in your life. Stop making excuses. Start saying you're sorry. Don't puke your pain onto others. Doing the necessary emotional, mental, physical, and spiritual work is not pleasant, but letting God, Jesus, and the Holy Spirit direct you are the only way we will move to the direction of our true purpose that God has for us in this world. Satan is here to destroy the wonderful plan that God has set out for us. Do not delay taking accountability for your life or the ones you love. Time is precious. And remember, this is not about perfection, this is about growing closer to Christ and God, so you feel peace and love.

What I have learned regarding perfection is that when I was in this belief system is that all I was doing was stressing myself and others out. I was putting myself in a pressure cooker all day long. This comes from the enemy, however some of the situations I found myself in were truly dysfunctional behaviors that people were presenting. That is why it is critical that we walk in love with one another. God did not put us on this planet to create sin and cause destruction with one another. He created us to bring love to one another. To work together and create miracles on this planet.

In closing, inspiring Navy Seal David Goggins gives a YouTube video "When I Meet God." In this video, he speaks that when he gets to heaven, God is getting ready to judge him. He explains that God has this paper, and He gives it to him. Goggins sees that is has all these amazing things on it. God explains to him that he went from 300 pounds to 185, became an amazing runner, was only the 36 African American to become a Navy seal, wrote a book that helped millions of people heal. David then looks at God and then says, this says David Goggins on it, but this isn't me. God says, this is what you should have been. You should have been this. God knows what you should be. Goggins goes onto explain that most of us take the easy way out. The choice that makes us feel good and they are not willing to break through their barriers. He explains that he visualized being judged by God in the end and that he wanted God being up there with a pen saying he did what God had written down, plus better to leave to the world so that God could be impressed by how he turned out. Goggins wanted to leave everything out on the table so there is nothing left to question in his life. Think about that. This is a profound idea that Goggins brings forth. How many of us give excuses every day or are afraid to be accountable to ourselves or others? As my good friend Jennifer, a former deliverance minister says in terms of close intimate relationships, "You can't give the rest of the world your best and the people closet to you the worst." So, get your act together and get accountable in Jesus Name!

Accountability Questions

1. What scares you about taking accountability for yourself?

2. What would your life look like if you started to take accountability for every area of your life?

3. If you knew you were going to die, how would you start to live your life differently? What areas of your life would you make changes too? How would you love yourself and others differently?

4. Where does the spirit of pride stop you from growing closer to others in your life? How does this keep you stunted on your Christ path?

5. What areas of life do you need forgiveness in toward yourself and others?

6. What stops you from taking accountability to renewing your mind in God's Word?

7.   What makes you feel justified in giving excuses for your unloving behaviors toward others instead of taking extreme ownership for them?

8.   What scares you the most about doing emotional work on yourself and taking accountability for the wounds and traumas that have been inflicted upon you from others?

9.   What stops you from taking steps to move toward Gods calling in your life?

10.   What stops you from having high quality relation-ships in your life?

11.   What stops you from holding your marriage as a covenant with God and with your spouse? Do you ever think that when you hurt them, you are really hurting yourself?

12.   What stops you from saying you're sorry and re-solving conflict with those you love before going to bed angry? Taking it one step further, what happens if you or the people you loved died the next day? What keeps you in the state of resistance to work through conflict in a more efficient manner? Time is the greatest illusion we have on Earth. What happens if you had this concept

in your mind? How would you live your life differently each day?

13. What stops you from taking time to rest quietly with God every day?

14. What stops you from taking the time to slow down and tell yourself and those that are most important to you that you love them daily?

15. What stops you from learning how to take authority over the enemy's influence in your life? Influence from the principalities and powers of this world is something that often goes unlooked. As the Holy Spirit on guidance of how to take authority over the enemy. This is an issue that is often overlooked in the problems we face.

16. What stops you from walking with God each day?

17. What stops you from uplifting others each day?

1

ROMANS 14:12

"So then each of you will give account of himself to God."

Day 1

2

JAMES 5:16

"Therefore confess your sins to one another and pray for one another, that you may be healed. The prayer of a righteous person has a great power as it is working."

_____

_____

_____

_____

_____

_____

_____

_____

_____

_____

_____

_____

_____

Day 2

3

GALATIANS 6:1-5

"Brothers, if anyone is caught in any transgression, you who are spiritual should restore him in a spirit of gentleness. Keep watch on yourself, lest you too be tempted. Be one another's burdens, and so fulfill the law of Christ. For if anyone thinks he is something, when he is nothing, he deceives himself. But let each one test his own work, and then his reason to boast will be in himself alone and not in his neighbor. For each will have to bear his own load."

_____

_____

_____

_____

_____

_____

_____

_____

Day 3

4

1 THESSALONIANS 5:11

"Therefore encourage one another and build another up.
just as you are doing."

_____

_____

_____

_____

_____

_____

_____

_____

_____

_____

_____

_____

_____

_____

Day 4

5

PROVERBS 27:17

"Iron Sharpens iron, and one man sharpens another."

_____

_____

_____

_____

_____

_____

_____

_____

_____

_____

_____

_____

_____

Day 5

6

LUKE 17:3

"Pay attention to yourselves? If your brother sins, rebuke him, and if he repents, forgive him."

_____

_____

_____

_____

_____

_____

_____

_____

_____

_____

_____

_____

_____

Day 6

7

MATTHEW 12:36-37

"I tell you, on the day of judgement people will give account for every careless word they speak, for by your words you will be justified, and by your words you will be condemned."

_____

_____

_____

_____

_____

_____

_____

_____

_____

_____

_____

_____

Day 7

8

ECCLESIASTES 4:9

"Two are better than one, because they have a good reward for their toil. For if they fall, one will lift up his fellow. But woe to him who is alone when he falls and has not another to life him up! Again, if two lie together, they keep warm, but how can one keep warm alone? And though a man might prevail against one who is alone, two will withstand him-a threefold cord is not quickly broken."

_____

_____

_____

_____

_____

_____

_____

_____

_____

_____

Day 8

9

JEREMIAH 17:10

"I the Lord search the heart and test the mind to give every man according to his ways, according to the fruit of his deeds."

_____

_____

_____

_____

_____

_____

_____

_____

_____

_____

_____

_____

_____

_____

Day 9

10

"Why do you see the speck that is in your brother's eye, but do not notice the log that is in your own eye? Or how can you say to your brother, 'Let me take the speck out of your eye;' when there is the log in your own eye? You hypocrite, first take the log out of your eye, and then you will see clearly to take the speck out of your brother's eye."

_____

_____

_____

_____

_____

_____

_____

_____

_____

_____

_____

Day 10

11

2 CORINTHIANS 5:10

"For we must all appear before the judgment seat of Christ, so that each one may receive what is due for what he has done in the body, whether good or evil."

_____

_____

_____

_____

_____

_____

_____

_____

_____

_____

_____

_____

_____

_____

Day 11

12

JAMES 4:17

"So whoever knows the right thing to do but fails to do it, to him this is sin."

_____

_____

_____

_____

_____

_____

_____

_____

_____

_____

_____

_____

_____

_____

Day 12

13

PROVERBS 12:15

"The way of a fool is right in his own eyes, but a wise man listens to advice."

_____

_____

_____

_____

_____

_____

_____

_____

_____

_____

_____

_____

_____

_____

Day 13

14

"Without counsel plans fail, but with many advisors they succeed."

_____

_____

_____

_____

_____

_____

_____

_____

_____

_____

_____

_____

_____

_____

Day 14

15

EPHESIANS 4:25

"Therefore, having put away falsehood, let each one of you speak the truth with his neighbor, for we are members of one another."

_____

_____

_____

_____

_____

_____

_____

_____

_____

_____

_____

_____

Day 15

16

GALATIANS 6:2

"Bear one another's burdens, and so fulfill the law of Christ."

_____

_____

_____

_____

_____

_____

_____

_____

_____

_____

_____

_____

_____

_____

_____

17

HEBREWS 10:25

"Not neglecting to meet together, as in the habit of some, but encouraging one another, and all the more as you see the day drawing near."

_____

_____

_____

_____

_____

_____

_____

_____

_____

_____

_____

_____

Day 17

_____

_____

_____

_____

_____

_____

_____

_____

_____

_____

_____

_____

_____

_____

_____

_____

_____

_____

_____

_____

18

COLOSSIANS 3:1

"If then you have been raised with Christ, seek the things that are above, where Christ is, seat-ed at the right hand of God. Set your mind on things that are above, not on things that are on earth."

_____

_____

_____

_____

_____

_____

_____

_____

_____

_____

_____

_____

Day 18

19

ROMANS 3:23

"For all have sinned and fallen short of the glory of God."

_____

_____

_____

_____

_____

_____

_____

_____

_____

_____

_____

_____

_____

_____

_____

Day 19

20

COLOSSIANS 3:16

"Let the word of Christ dwell in you richly, teaching and admonishing one another in all wisdom, singing psalms and hymns and spiritual songs, with thankfulness in your hearts to God."

_____

_____

_____

_____

_____

_____

_____

_____

_____

_____

_____

_____

Day 20

21

JAMES 1:19

"Know this, my beloved brothers, let every person be quick
to hear, slow to speak, slow to anger."

_____

_____

_____

_____

_____

_____

_____

_____

_____

_____

_____

_____

_____

_____

Day 21

22

EPHESIANS 5:21

"Submitting to one another out of reverence for Christ."

_____

_____

_____

_____

_____

_____

_____

_____

_____

_____

_____

_____

_____

_____

_____

Day 22

23

HEBREWS 10:24

"Let us consider how to stir up one another to love and good works."

_____

_____

_____

_____

_____

_____

_____

_____

_____

_____

_____

_____

_____

_____

Day 23

24

JAMES 5:19-20

"My brothers, if anyone among you wanders from the truth and someone brings him back, let him know that whoever brings back a sinner from his wandering will save his soul from death and will cover a multitude of sins."

_____

_____

_____

_____

_____

_____

_____

_____

_____

_____

_____

_____

Day 24

25

ROMANS 14:10

"Why do you pass judgment on your brother? Or you, why
do you despise your brother? For we will stand before the
judgment seat of God."

_____

_____

_____

_____

_____

_____

_____

_____

_____

_____

_____

_____

_____

Day 25

26

ECCLESIASTES 11:9

"Rejoice, O young man, in your youth, and let your heart cheer you in the days of your youth. Walk in the ways of your heart and the sight of your eyes. But know that for all these things God will bring you into judgment."

_____

_____

_____

_____

_____

_____

_____

_____

_____

_____

_____

_____

Day 26

27

ROMANS 12:15

"Rejoice with those who rejoice; weep with those who weep."

_____

_____

_____

_____

_____

_____

_____

_____

_____

_____

_____

_____

_____

_____

_____

Day 27

28

1 John 3:17-21

"But if anyone has the world's good and see his brother in needs, yet closes his heart against him, how does God's love abide in him? Little children, let us not love in word or talk but in deed and in truth. By this we shall know that we are of the truth and reassure our heart be-fore him; for whenever our condemns us, God is greater than our heart, and he knows every-thing. Beloved, if our heart does not condemn us, we have confidence before God."

_____

_____

_____

_____

_____

_____

_____

_____

_____

Day 28

29

GENESIS 2:18

"The Lord God said, "It is not good that man should be alone, I will make him a helper fit for him."

_____

_____

_____

_____

_____

_____

_____

_____

_____

_____

_____

_____

_____

Day 29

30

ROMANS 12:1

"I appeal to you therefore, brothers, by the mercies of God, to present your bodies as a living sacrifice, holy and acceptable to God, which is your spiritual worship."

_____

_____

_____

_____

_____

_____

_____

_____

_____

_____

_____

_____

_____

Day 30

CPSIA information can be obtained
at www.ICGtesting.com
Printed in the USA
LVHW081910270821
696280LV00002B/273